Written by: Angela Pearse

Edited by: Bruno Luis

Contents

Introduction to England

A nation of tea drinkers, cucumber sandwich eaters and football lovers, the English proffer a bewildering array of accents and dialects that make you wonder if you actually understand the language at all. But there's nowhere in world that does history quite like England. If the romance of medieval castles, the innovation of the Industrial Revolution and music of The Beatles appeals, then you've come to the right place.

With its town planning and roads firmly laid by the Romans, you'll find some of the best architectural examples of this period in cities such as Bath, Chester, York and even London. England takes great pride in its past, and with organisations like the National Trust and English Heritage on the scene you can be assured of top-class visitor centres, exhibitions and facilities.

But don't just visit the main cities of England, the idyllic countryside in places such as Suffolk and the Cotswolds isn't just a myth. Rolling fields of waving wheat, thatched-roof cottages and Tudor taverns really do exist. Join us as we explore England from top to toe, from shore to shore, outlining 20 of the best places to visit in this incredibly diverse country.

#1 London

London is England's capital city and a world leader of industry, finance, education, entertainment, and fashion plus many other sectors. As a tourist destination, London boasts a heady mix of historical and cultural attractions that has earned it the title of the 'world's most visited city'. Luckily London also has the world's largest airport system to cater to all the inbound visitors, and one of world's largest underground train networks, commonly known as the Tube. Some of London's most popular historic landmarks include: Buckingham Palace, the Tower of London, Big Ben, and Westminster Abbey, while more recent ones such as the Millennium Dome and London Eye, just as easily draw the crowds.

London's earliest origins are still the subject of some debate but it is known that a major Roman settlement called Londinium existed in the 2nd century AD on the banks of the River Thames. The settlement consisted of around 60,000 people and this ancient core, with its city walls still apparent in sections, is today known as the City of London. After the Romans departed, Londinium fell into disuse until the Anglo-Saxons took it over in the 5th century, named it

Lundenwic and used it as a trading port.

The Norman Conquest of 1066 changed London's fortunes dramatically. William the Conqueror, as the new King of England, built the Tower of London, which was to feature largely in the city's landscape for centuries as a royal residence and feared prison. Of all the major royal figures in London's history, the long reign of Queen Elizabeth I from 1558 to 1603 is perhaps the most important as it paved the way for London to be an international powerhouse, especially in the arts. During this period, one of the greatest writers the world has ever known came to the fore, William Shakespeare, whose plays and poems are as popular today as they were in the 16th century.

Anyone interested in William Shakespeare's legacy should visit the Globe Theatre in Southwark. This is a modern reconstruction of the original 16th century theatre, complete with Tudor walls and a thatched roof, where you can see Shakespeare productions all year round. World Heritage Site, the Tower of London on the opposite side of the Thames is a must-visit. To get there you can walk across Tower Bridge, one of the city's iconic landmarks.

Allow at least three hours, if not more, at the Tower of London, and take a tour with a Beefeater guide to make the most of the experience. Afterwards art lovers will appreciate some of the finest exhibition spaces in the world with the National Gallery and Tate Modern topping the list, and where else can you find more treasures from around the world than the British Museum?

© Flickr / André Zehetbauer

Big Ben & Houses of Parliament

London is renowned for its nightlife, especially theatres in the districts of Leicester Square and Soho. Sightseeing in London can make for weary feet but with eight royal parks to relax in, including Hyde Park, St James's Park and Kensington Gardens, you'll soon be ready for the next round of London's delights.

#2 Manchester

© Wikimedia / Pete Birkinshaw

Manchester is one of England's largest cities, and as the home of the Industrial Revolution, is one of the country's most popular tourist destinations. With its numerous historical and cultural attractions, as well as an eclectic mix of bars and restaurants, there's plenty to experience in this vibrant city. Dominating the north of England with an urban area of over 2.5 million people, Manchester today is as hardworking and innovative as ever. Manchester Airport serves both domestic and international flights, and the city has an extensive train, tram and bus network.

Manchester started out as Mamucium, a Roman Fort built in 79 AD to defend against the Brigantes, a Celtic tribe who existed at the same time in Northern England. Some of the foundations of this original fort can still be seen in the suburb of Castlefield. After the Romans departed, Manchester was ruled by the Saxons and the Normans.

During the 14th century a significant number of Flemish weavers settled in the city and paved the way for what would become the world's first manufacturing city.

Manchester's textile industry was the catalyst of the Industrial Revolution in the 18th century, with its cotton cloth such a sought after commodity that the town was overrun with cotton mills and processing factories. This economic and population boom in turn inspired new technologies and innovations by engineering firms such as, superior machinery, chemical processes and an extensive railway network. Manchester's wartime production of bombs, planes and military vehicles made it a target for the German Luftwaffe airforce who bombed it extensively. Regeneration and rebuilding are an ongoing part of the Manchester urban landscape, with many of the older industrial areas being transformed into trendy inner city bars, restaurants and shopping areas.

The city once dubbed 'Cottonopolis' now sports an edgy vibe with an astonishing revamp of cotton warehouses and factories remade into trendy apartments,

such as those in the Northern Quarter. Manchester flaunts its fascinating heritage as a tourist attraction with guided tours of areas like Ancoats, which sported the world's first industrial workshops. Here you can peep into the past via brass eyeholes set up at various sites to view artefacts and structures from the industrial period.

Manchester Town Hall

Manchester has always been at the heart of British politics, and you can learn more at the People's Museum, or if art and science are more your thing, take in The Lowry or the Museum of Science and Industry. Some of the coolest bars to enjoy a drink in Manchester include the Apotheca, Epernay, The Alchemist, Cloud 23 and the Hula Tiki Lounge.

#3 York

© Flickr / Michael D Beckwith

York boasts the title of being England's best preserved medieval city and is ringed by Roman walls. Located at the conjunction of the River Ouse and River Foss in the northeast, it is the capital of the county of Yorkshire.

York has been at the forefront of many of England's major events and has plenty of historic attractions to suit all ages and interests. The most iconic of these is York Minster, a magnificent Gothic-style cathedral in the heart of the city.

The city first started out as a Roman fort in 71 AD and was called Eboracum. It went on to become the capital town of Northumbria and a major market place and wool trading centre. Early York featured a sturdy rectangle of walls as part of the fort's defences.

Today, the ten-sided Multangular Tower situated in the Museum

Gardens is the most complete structure that remains from the Roman walls. The walls stretch for almost three and half kilometres around the city and can be walked upon. Apart from the Roman influence, York's architecture features Viking and Saxon ruins and, more recently, buildings from the Georgian and Edwardian era.

York's importance as a trading centre and defence of northern England made it a target for Scottish invaders, and the most notable occurrence was the Siege of York in 1644. An enduring reminder of York's embattled past is York Castle, first built by William the Conqueror in 1068 it is now a public tourist attraction affording excellent views of the city.

York invites visitors to step back in time and discover its two millennia of history. This is the perfect place for both young and old with loads of fun activities and historic ambience. You'll fall in love with York's quaint streets, like The Shambles, York's oldest. Once home to 25 butcher's shops, today The Shambles is lined with trendy boutiques, gift shops and cafes. Boasting one of Britain's most vibrant beer scenes York has over 250 pubs, with the oldest being the Ye Olde Starre Inne and supposedly the most haunted, The Golden Fleece.

York Minster

Museums abound with popular ones being the JORVIK Viking Centre, a nod to York's Scandinavian past with a reconstructed Viking settlement and animated models, and York Castle Museum with collections covering prehistoric times, through to the space age.

York Minster is a must-see as Britain's largest gothic cathedral, highlights include taking a free tour, the view from the central tower and the interactive undercroft area.

#4 Liverpool

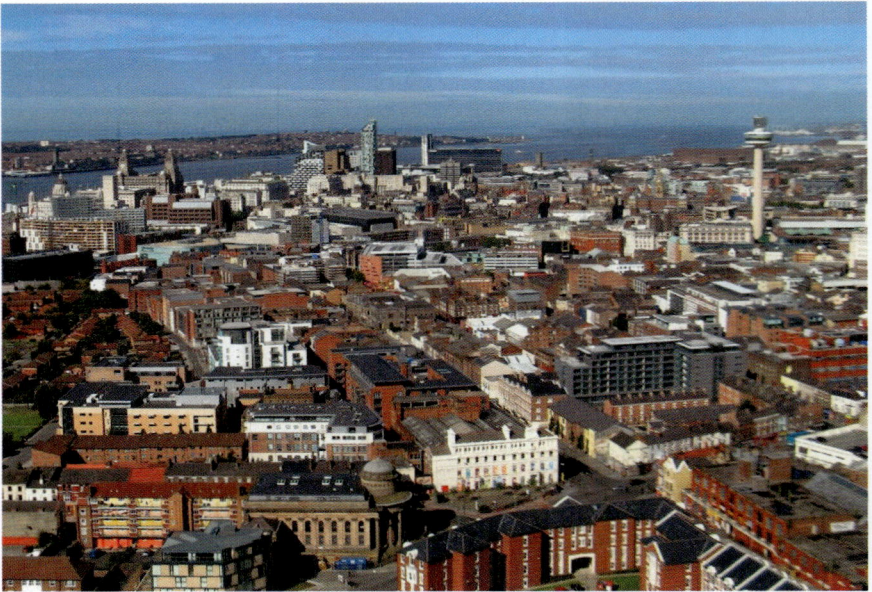

Liverpool, located in Merseyside in the northwest of England, is a major port city and has UNESCO World Heritage attractions. It is best known as the home of the music group 'The Beatles' who took the world by storm in the 1960s. Today many visitors travel to Liverpool to discover the history of the 'Fab Four' and see associated landmarks such as Strawberry Fields and Penny Lane. Residents of Liverpool are commonly known in the UK as 'Scousers' and the Scouse accent is very distinctive making the people and attractions of Liverpool a unique corner of England to visit.

Liverpool as a city was slow to grow, with a population of only 500 by the mid-16th century. In the Middle Ages it was a trading town and a port but the first commercial dock wasn't built until 1715. This was to accommodate the slave ships and trade coming from Africa and the West Indies. Subsequently the town became prosperous and started to grow because of the slave trade. In turn the city's architecture started reflecting its wealth with major buildings being constructed and along with Manchester, it had railway links in the early 19th century.

Liverpool's population grew rapidly during this period taking in hundreds of thousands of Irish migrants escaping the Great Famine. Still more immigrants arrived during the 19th and 20th centuries from around Europe. Liverpool was a cultural melting pot with Greek, German, Nordic and Polish communities, to name a few, springing up all across the city. After World War II, Liverpool also became home for many displaced immigrants and has a significant Jewish community. During the 1960s Liverpool was in the limelight for its Merseybeat music, which produced supergroup The Beatles, along with other rock bands. It holds the Guinness World Record for being the World Capital City of Pop, with 56 number one singles.

Beatles fans will make a beeline for the main Fab Four attractions in Liverpool which should begin with the 'Beatles Story', an exhibition which gives the complete history of the group.

This is in Albert Dock, part of the UNESCO World Heritage area on the waterfront. You can also join the Magical Mystery Tour here, a bus trip around the city taking two hours and pointing out different landmarks associated with The Beatles. A major Beatles attraction is the Cavern Club, situated on Matthew Street where the group first rose to fame, this is still used today for live music acts. There are also tours of the homes of John Lennon and Paul McCartney run by the National Trust.

© Wikimedia / David Poblador i Garcia

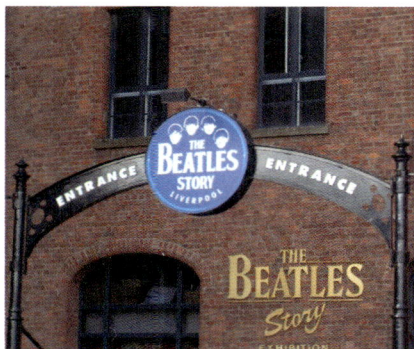

The Beatles Story Exhibition

Apart from its Beatles attractions, Liverpool has the most museums and art galleries of any city in the UK, apart from London. Some of the best ones are the Tate Liverpool, the FACT centre, the Walker Art Gallery and Sudley House.

#5 Stonehenge

The prehistoric monument Stonehenge is one of the most famous attractions in England and a UNESCO World Heritage Site. Located near the villages Amesbury and Salisbury in Wiltshire, it consists of a circle of standing stones, mostly upright, which have been dated between 3000 BC and 2000 BC.

The entire area around Amesbury and Salisbury is of archaeological significance for its Neolithic monuments and earthworks. A recently built visitor centre has made Stonehenge more accessible for tourists with amenities, exhibits and information about the site.

Although it is one of the best-known prehistoric monuments in Europe, the significance behind Stonehenge still remains a mystery. Due to the fact that the people who erected the stones left no written record, there have been many theories and debate to its purpose over the years. One such theory is that it was a burial site and evidence of cremated human remains discovered supports this. Others propose it was an astronomical observatory, a religious site, or more recently, a place of healing.

Supernatural theories also abound as to how the massive stones were transported to the site. Whatever the practical reasons for its existence, Stonehenge has always been associated with rituals and today still attracts mystics and pagan worshippers who come to the site at certain times of the year.

If you're not a pagan worshipper but simply wish to visit Stonehenge, then the visitor centre is your first port of call. Situated approximately one mile from Stonehenge itself, this is where you can catch the shuttle bus up to the stones, stock up on information about the site and grab lunch or a snack if you need to. This is a popular attraction so visits to the stones are by pre-booked ticket for certain time slots.

If you're visiting independently the best times to book your tickets for are first thing in the morning or late afternoon, to avoid the tour buses from London. The closest you will be able to get to the stones is about 10 metres, as the inner core is roped off.

© Wikimedia / Simon Wakefield

Sunset at Stonehenge

However if you're really keen, there are Special Access visits at dawn or in the evening lasting an hour which let you to walk amongst the stones.

#6 Lake District

Photo by DAVID ILIFF. License: CC-BY-SA 3.0

Situated in the north west of England in Cumbria is the popular holiday spot known as the Lake District. This scenic national park is a mountainous region offering hill and forest treks, many small villages to explore, cultural events and numerous lakes. Two of these, Wastwater and Windermere, are the deepest and longest in England.

The Lake District region itself is relatively large at nearly 2,300 square kilometres and the highest of its mountains (or 'fells' as the locals call them) is Scafell Pike at 978 metres. Part of the Lake District is owned by the National Trust but, apart from restricted access to cultivated land, the public routes are completely free to roam and explore at your leisure.

The Lake District is the most visited of all the national parks in England. Its beauty has long been recorded in novels, poetry and paintings, particularly during the 18th and 19th centuries with famous English writers, such as Wordsworth, who lived there. Other poets and writers such as Shelley, Keats and Tennyson and many more, visited the region on a number of occasions and were inspired by the scenery and the character of the villages. Many of the local words and phrases, such as 'tarn' meaning a small lake and 'fell' a mountain were used in their literature.

More recently, children's author Beatrix Potter based her hugely successful Peter Rabbit books on the animals she encountered as a child on holiday in the Lake District in the early 20th century. Hill Top Farm where she lived is now a museum open to the public.

If you're visiting the Lake District for the first time then you're best to start at the Lake District Visitor Centre called 'Brockhole'. This is set on the shore of Lake Windermere, and you can get an overview of all that's on offer, as well as expert help on local events and where to stay. Try a cosy holiday cottage or quirky but

friendly bed and breakfast, or treat yourself to a stay in a luxury hotel.

The Village of Glenridding and Ullswater in the Lake District

Depending on your interests, you'll find plenty to keep you busy from guided walks and cycling, to shopping and afternoon tea. As Beatrix Potter noted, the Lake District is home for a variety of wildlife, so it is a paradise for animal lovers.

Keep a look out for red squirrels, the Lake District is an important sanctuary for them, and it also features numerous species of birds.

#7 Cornwall

© Wikimedia / Jim Champion

England's most southwesterly point is the peninsula of Cornwall, known for its magnificent 300 mile coastline, excellent surfing and delicious cream teas. It has a number of iconic attractions such as Minack Theatre, Tintagel Castle, the Eden Project and the Lost Gardens of Heligan.

Cornwall is easily accessible from London and other parts of the United Kingdom, with daily rail services to Truro or St Austell, the two largest towns. There are also airports at Newquay and Exeter to make your journey there even quicker.

Cornwall has a distinct character all its own reflected by its history and language. Many of its towns and villages have names derived from the Cornish language which has its roots from the Celts. Their legacy can still be seen dotted across the region with Celtic crosses, granite burial chambers and holy wells.

Traditionally Cornish people are known for their genuine warmth and hospitality, so you can expect generous helpings of Cornish pasties (a meat pie) and Cornish cream teas (tea with scones, cream and jam).

The Cornish have always been hardworking, with tin mining being an important part of the economy during the Middle Ages through to the 19th century. Since the region is almost entirely made up of coastline, you'll find many traditional villages still reliant on pilchard fishing for their livelihood. Cornwall also has a large dairy farming industry and its vegetable crops flourish in the mild climate.

Parts of Cornwall have been designated as Areas of Outstanding Natural Beauty including the protected wild moorland of Bodmin Moor, as well as several stretches of the coastline that make up the South West Coast Path. This dramatic pathway is a popular hiking route, and can be broken up into walks lasting a day, several days or a week, depending on your schedule. There are many bed and breakfasts situated along to the way, either up on the clifftop or in tiny fishing harbours.

The Eden Project

If you're after more of a city vibe then Truro will deliver, with boutique clothing shops and art galleries nestled alongside museums and historic churches.

The market town of St Austell is a perfect base for a visit to the Eden Project, a vast futuristic domed garden, or the Lost Gardens of Heligan, an extensive garden estate given new life after it fell into disrepair during World War II.

#8 Bath

Southwest England is home to the county of Somerset, and particularly the city of Bath. This Georgian spa town is a World Heritage Site, and apart from its archaeological significance, offers tourists much in the way of cultural and entertainment options.

With its museums, theatres and sporting venues, Bath should definitely be on your list for best places to visit in England.

The Celts were first to settle the area around 1 AD and built a shrine to the goddess Sulis. Then came the Romans in 60 AD who built the first bath houses and called the town Aquae Sulis. Most of the bath houses fell into disrepair after the Romans left Britain, though there is a well preserved example of a Roman bath complex still in existence.

This has been modified somewhat with several architectural structures added in later centuries.

Today the original Roman Baths are situated below street level and feature the Roman Temple, Sacred Spring and Roman Bath House.

The Roman Baths are not safe to swim in due to lead pipes and water quality, so visitors can only admire. The museum at the site is well worth a visit, as is the Grand Pump Room, an historic building next door where you can sample the waters (said to have healing powers) as well as partake of afternoon tea.

Photo by DAVID ILIFF. License: CC-BY-SA 3.0

The Roman Baths

It would be strange to visit a city called Bath, without actually bathing. Luckily, since the Roman Baths are off limits, the nearby Thermae Bath Spa will take care of your needs in that respect.

A blend of historic and contemporary design, this natural spa features an indoor Minerva Bath as well as an open-air rooftop pool. You can also choose from an array of spa treatments.

While on your spa break in Bath, be sure to check out the Building of Bath Collection which displays information on the formation of the city during the 18th century.

This was when all the lovely Georgian buildings, many of which are now hotels, restaurants and pubs, were constructed. You can also discover the architectural highlights of Bath on an open bus tour or a guided tour on foot.

#9 Birmingham

© Wikimedia / JimmyGuano

The second largest city in England, Birmingham is a major commercial centre with many cultural institutions. Situated in the West Midlands area, the city is known for its influence in art, music, literature and food.

But don't go thinking this is just a concrete jungle, Birmingham has award winning urban parks, cruisy canals and cycle routes, perfect for a breather before continuing your exploration of this lively and exciting destination.

You'll know you're in Birmingham as soon as you hear the distinctive local 'Brummie' accent and dialect. 'Brummie' comes from the city's nickname of 'Brum' which has its roots in earlier dialect names. Birmingham was a prominent Anglo-Saxon settlement, and then a largish market town in the medieval period.

But it wasn't until the Industrial Revolution in the 18th century that it became a world leader, along with Manchester, in textile manufacturing and paved the way for many advances in science and technology.

After being heavily bombed during World War II, extensive redevelopments of the city took place in the 1950s and 1960s. At this time Birmingham was also at the forefront of the British music scene which led to globally recognised bands such as Led Zeppelin in the 1970s and Duran Duran in the 1980s.

Today with a wide range of music venues catering for all kinds of local and international acts you can rock 'til your hearts content in Birmingham.

Birmingham is a city on the move, with many of its old industrial areas being transformed and restored, such as Brindleyplace and The Mailbox, and now home to upmarket shops, bars and restaurants. There are many heritage attractions including the Jewellery Quarter which has over 400 working jewellery businesses, the largest concentration in Europe.

Birmingham Museum and Art Gallery

You can learn more about this 'City of a Thousand Trades' at the Birmingham Museum & Art Gallery showcasing how the city produced everything from pens and buckles, to buttons and guns.

Chocolate was also a major production in Birmingham from the 19th century. Today Cadbury World is a popular family attraction where you can learn about the manufacturing process, go on action rides, chill out at the 4D cinema and, of course, stock up on chocolate.

#10 Cotswolds

© Wikimedia / Saffron Blaze

One of the most picturesque rural areas in England is the Cotswolds, situated in the central south of the country. Featuring the stunning Cotswold Hills, rolling fields, characterful stone-built villages and magnificent stately homes, the Cotswolds is England's largest designated Area of Outstanding Beauty.

A favourite destination for holidaymakers, especially in the warmer months, the Cotswolds landscape is ideal for those keen on hiking, cycling and lots of fresh country air.

There are around 40 towns and villages in the Cotswolds, including the larger border towns of Bath, Gloucester and Cheltenham, with the area covering parts of several counties including Oxfordshire, Warwickshire and Somerset.

Historically the area has been settled since the Stone Age, with a period of occupation by the Romans who built the town of Gloucester and also roads.

However, it was the rise of the wool trade during the Middle Ages that gave the area its greatest prosperity. During this time, as in other parts of the country, a number of stone churches were built with the profits from wool trading, earning them the name 'wool churches'.

Most of the villages in the Cotswolds are also made out of this Cotswold stone, famous for its golden colour attributed to Jurassic fossils in the limestone. You can still find small stone quarries, such as Castle Rock on Cleeve Hill, which are today used for rock climbing.

Spring and summer are the best times to visit the Cotswolds, when the countryside is at its loveliest. One of the reasons that international visitors especially are captivated by the area is because it is so typically English, with beech trees, meadows, castles and traditional villages.

The attractions in the Cotswolds are many and varied but some of the must-see highlights include, the ancient market town of Chipping Campden, Sudeley Castle & Gardens, Warwick Castle and Gloucester Cathedral.

© Wikimedia / Saffron Blaze

Gloucester Cathedral

If you're staying for more than a day (highly recommended) then you'll be able to explore many of the walking trails and cycle paths in the area, stop for lunch in the village pubs and browse the foodie markets.

There's always something happening in the Cotswolds with sporting events and festivals taking place throughout the year.

#11 Brighton

© Wikimedia /Bojan Lazarevic

Bustling Brighton is just an hour from London by direct train, making it one of the most popular places for a day trip out of the city. Situated on the southern coast England, Brighton offers a pebbled beach (with free deck chairs), safe swimming for children and amusement arcades.

Some of the most iconic attractions associated with the town include, Brighton Rock, the Brighton Wheel and Brighton Pier.

With its numerous pubs and night clubs, the town is also hot spot for weekend party goers from London.

Archaeological evidence has been discovered that suggests the Romans settled in Brighton in the 1st century AD, built villas and farmed the area. Later the Celts and Anglo-Saxons both had periods of occupation and the town was called 'Brighthelmstone' in medieval times.

During the early 18th century, the fad of sea bathing and drinking seawater if you were ill was a popular notion, so Brighton turned into a health resort.

Later, the original fishing village gave way to Georgian terraced houses and Brighton not only became a fashionable place to visit if you needed some bracing sea air, but a nice place to live as well.

A regular visitor of the town was King George IV, who improved the architecture and patronised the construction of the Royal Pavilion. When the railway was built in 1841 the seaside resort became accessible as a day trip from London.

Brighton's mild climate and propensity for sunshine, means it can get busy at weekends during the summer months, especially if there's a heatwave. If you want to experience a calmer side of Brighton without the crowds, especially on Brighton Pier, then visit on a weekday or in the off season.

For those who like sandy beaches, Brighton's pebbled affair will disappoint but at nearly nine

kilometres long there's room enough to spread out.

© Wikimedia /Jenni Ahonen

Brighton Pier

Brighton's attractions cater to a wide range of people; couples, families, groups, and is known for its gay friendly attitude towards locals and visitors.

The seafront area between Hove and Brighton Marina is a must-stroll, while North Laine is awash with quirky shops and The Lanes is the best place to go for upmarket shopping, restaurants, nightclubs and bars.

#12 Devon

© Dietmar Rabich, rabich.de, CC BY-SA 4.0, Wikimedia Commons

Situated in the southwest of England between Cornwall and Somerset, Devon is a sought after holiday spot. The historic port of Plymouth is the largest city, while Exeter is the main administrative center.

Devon has excellent weather, and the south coast towns, such as Torbay and Brixham, enjoy lots of sunshine hours earning this part of Devon the nickname 'English Riviera'. The county is known for its delicious Devonshire cream teas and cider but with two large national parks, Dartmoor and Exmoor, both offer opportunities for working off any excess while on holiday.

With periods of occupation by both the Romans and the Normans, Devon's past is firmly rooted in agriculture and labour. Tin mining, as well farming, were the mainstays of the economy during the Middle Ages, when the land was owned by the country gentry.

But weather conditions plus bouts of plague and smallpox, made it difficult for people to sustain a living and many emigrated. In the 19th century the climate improved, with long hot summers attracting more and more tourists, and

Devon was made more accessible with the building of the railway. Today, tourism is the main sector of Devon's economy, with agriculture, fishing and manufacturing also important livelihoods.

Getting to Devon is easy with the Exeter International Airport serving flights from other parts of the UK and Europe. The train service is also excellent with a regular timetable from London's Paddington Station, as well as to and from other regions.

The populations of Devon's coastal resorts swell in the summer months, with towns such as Torquay, Brixham, Exmouth and Sidmouth receiving an influx of holidaymakers attracted by the clean beaches, safe swimming, quaint shops and restaurants.

© Wikimedia / David Dixon

Harbor of Brixham

There are also many rural market towns, including Honiton, Okehampton, Tavistock and Barnstaple each with their own individual character, where you can stay in a thatched cottage, buy speciality foods, visit farmers markets and browse for antiques and art.

For those wanting an active holiday, the South West Coast Path runs along both coastlines, Dartmoor and Exmoor National Parks have scenic hiking, and Bideford Bay is one of the top surf spots in Britain.

#13 Cambridge

© Flickr / Chris Huang

The university city of Cambridge is situated in the east of England and can be reached in just under an hour by train from London. This ease of access and its reputation of having one of the top universities in the world means Cambridge is a year round tourist destination.

Iconic Cambridge activities including punting on the River Cam, live theatre productions, and tours of the historic College buildings. There are 31 Colleges in total and most of these are open for public visits.

Cambridge is an ancient city whose occupation goes back to prehistoric times. Archaeological evidence shows smalls settlements during the Iron Age and widespread farmsteads during the time of the Romans up to the 4th century AD.

It was the Viking rule in the 9th century AD, however, that had the most influence on the city's growth due to their extensive trading activity. The next significant period of growth came in the 19th century with increased agricultural production, although Cambridge wasn't officially named a city until 1951.

Cambridge played an instrumental part in World War II, being an important centre for defence of the east coast of England, as an evacuation centre for London and as a military center.

The R.A.F training center and headquarters were based here but no major bombing raids occurred. It was at Cambridge's Trinity College that military leaders met and the plans were laid for the allied invasion of Europe known as D-Day.

For the curious, Cambridge offers a sneak peek at English academic life, with its formal college grounds, plethora of bookshops, student pubs and a lazy winding river perfect for testing your punting skills.

King's College Chapel which dominates the Cambridge skyline, along with St John's College Chapel tower, has the largest fan vault ceiling in the world and stunning stained glass windows; during term time the choir sings Evensong daily.

© Wikimedia / Andrew Dunn

King's College Chapel

As well as the Colleges being open for visits, so are the university's nine museums and accompanying collections, including the must-see Fitzwilliam Museum, intriguing Whipple Museum of the History of Science, and fascinating Polar Museum.

Setting out on foot is the best way to explore Cambridge's historic market place, take in one of the city tours during the day or a ghost walk at night.

#14 Blackpool

The resort town of Blackpool has been a fashionable place for Brits to holiday since the early 20th century. Situated in the northwest of England in Lancashire, today Blackpool is as popular as ever for its beaches, fun fair rides, amusement arcades, lighting shows and entertainment events.

Packed to the brim with year round attractions, restaurants, pubs and nightclubs, it's the town of choice for hen and stag parties, group getaways and family holidays.

No one would have guessed that Blackpool would become an entertainment mecca during the Middle Ages. Then just a small coastal hamlet, it remained a bit of a backwater until the mid-18th century.

At this point it was all the rage in England to travel to the coast during summer for a dose of sea water bathing and fresh air to get healthy. Blackpool became in vogue and it grew even more so when the railway was built in the 1840s.

The railway not only made the town more accessible, it was cheaper to get there. By 1881 Blackpool had blossomed into a major seaside resort with a promenade, pubs, fish and chip shops and of course, donkey rides, it even had fortune tellers.

Today, the town's economy is mainly reliant on tourism and with millions of visitors annually this shows no sign of slowing.

Vestiges of Blackpool's heritage can be found with attractions such as the historic tramway, Blackpool Tower and the three Victorian piers constructed in the 19th century which are home to various rides, theatres, bars and restaurants.

Pleasure Beach is the name of the theme park on the seafront and this has recently been voted the best theme park in the UK. It has almost 40 rides and attractions, together with 10 roller coasters

and a myriad of thrill rides and water rides.

Blackpool Tower

It's not all adrenaline pumping fun at Blackpool, it does have quieter activities such as beautiful gardens and sandy beaches, the South Promenade ideal for strolling and checking out art work, and many independent retailers.

For night life though Blackpool is hard to beat with its lively pubs, multi-leveled nightclubs, music acts and the famous Blackpool Illuminations, a magical festival lighting up the promenade in autumn.

#15 Norfolk

© Wikimedia / summonedbyfells

Norfolk is a mainly rural county in the east of England, characterized by low-lying farmland, coastal towns and a network of rivers known as The Broads. In recent years, Norfolk has become more popular as a tourist destination as people seek more remote, untouched areas of England for short breaks.

Norfolk in that respect has plenty of breathing room, being one of the least populated places in the country. Norwich is the main city of Norfolk and has been designated a UNESCO City of Literature for its long history of publishing.

Norfolk and farming have always gone hand-in-hand, with the area early on being occupied by the Romans who set up homesteads, ports and roads. Sheep rearing and salt production were the main production industries at this time. Evidence of Roman defence fortifications built in the 3rd century AD against the Saxons can be seen with ruins such as Burgh Castle, and forts at Brancaster on the north coast and Caister-on-Sea on the east coast.

In the 5th century AD, after the Romans departed, the Angles, a Germanic people, took over the region which eventually became known as East Anglia. They split into two distinct groups, hence 'north folk' (Norfolk) and 'south folk' (Suffolk).

Norfolk became most prosperous during the Middle Ages with increased agriculture and wool trading – it has the greatest number of wool churches in Great Britain, 659. Norfolk in the 20th century was an important airfield base for both World Wars, and a significant contributor to the country's agricultural production, and it remains so today.

In terms of a tourist destination, Norfolk has many holiday attractions. The seaside resorts of Great Yarmouth, Holkham and Cromer have some of the finest beaches you'll find in England. Many stretches of this unspoilt coastline are protected bird sanctuaries and national parks. The peaceful Norfolk Broads are

popular with boaties, and also offer walking and cycling trails.

© Wikimedia / Norfolkadam

Great Yarmouth

Explore the gentle inland countryside dotted with forest pines, and stately homes. West Norfolk and The Fens are best for family outdoor activities, while the south has a typical English countryside, village pubs and historic sites.

For more heritage, culture and shopping, Norwich is a must-visit. Don't forget to keep a look out for some unique local food specialities such as the Norfolk treacle tart, Cromer crabs, Brancaster mussels, and Colman's mustard.

#16 Suffolk

© Wikimedia / Squeezyboy

Suffolk lies just beneath Norfolk in the east of England. The Suffolk Coast has been designated an Area of Outstanding Natural Beauty and its picturesque rural countryside has been celebrated by famous English painters John Constable and Thomas Gainsborough.

Just a short distance from London by train and road, Suffolk is a popular short break destination for anyone looking to escape the big city. Ipswich is the main county town in the south of Suffolk, but other popular places to stay include Bury St Edmunds or Newmarket in the north and Lowestoft on the coast.

Many archaeological finds, such as axes, spearheads, armour and swords have been found in West Suffolk, suggesting that occupation of the area was continuous from the Stone Age through to the Bronze Age. East Suffolk has a major site dated to the Anglo-Saxon period, known as Sutton Hoo. Here a ship burial has yielded precious objects, like gold and silver bowls, musical instruments and jewellery.

Like Norfolk, Suffolk's fortunes have coincided closely with the land since ancient times, and today there are wide range of farms to be found producing all kinds of crops from wheat and linseed, to beans and oats.

The Suffolk Show held in Ipswich in May is the annual showcasing of produce from the region. Although much of the coastline is protected, the soft rocks it's made of are subject to continual erosion, and several towns are under threat.

The Suffolk Coast & Heaths has been designated an Area of Outstanding Natural Beauty, and is a good focal point for any trip to the county.

Consisting of 60 miles of coastline encompassing shingle beaches, heathland and small coastal villages, it also features three long distance walking trails: the Sandlings Walk, the Suffolk Coast Path and the Stour & Orwell Walk. The last connects with the Stour Valley Path, which takes

walkers through an area known as 'Constable Country'.

© Wikimedia / Dave Briggs

Framlingham Castle

Slow travel via walking, cycling and horseriding is recommended so you don't miss out on the charming characteristics of Suffolk, like thatched cottages, historic churches and stately homes that you may come across unexpectedly and wish to explore.

But there are community buses that are a convenient way to get from town to town if you don't wish to drive. Places to stay in Suffolk that have good transport links include Bury St. Edmonds, Lavenham and Sudbury.

#17 Chester

© Wikimedia / Tagishsimon

Chester is an English border city lying close to Wales in the northwest of England. The city's architecture is predominantly medieval and Victorian, and it is almost completely ringed by Roman walls. These are Grade I listed and the most well-preserved in Britain.

The city features a mix of heritage and modern attractions, and England's magnificent North Country is at hand for visitors wishing to explore further afield. The closest airport to Chester is Liverpool John Lennon Airport, just over half an hour's drive away and the town has good rail links with the south, east and north of the country.

The origins of Chester began in 79 AD with the Romans who created a defensive fort and named it Deva Victrix. Central Chester has four main roads, Northgate, Watergate,

Bridgegate and Eastgate whose layout dates from this period.

After the Romans, the Saxons settled at Chester, strengthening and extending its walls to keep out the Danish. Eventually the city fell under the control of invading Normans, but was one of the last towns in England to do so.

The town was almost destroyed by fire in the 13th century and the subsequent rebuilding led to the creation of the Chester Rows, covered walkways with shops and commercial properties on two levels.

The Chester Rows are one of the unique tourist attractions of the city, another is Chester's black and white Victorian architecture which was part of a 19th century Tudor Revival.

The main attraction in Chester is its impressive walls which encircle the city and form a three kilometre tourist walk. Next to the section of wall from Newgate to the River Dee are the Roman Gardens which have a number of Roman artefacts, as does the Grosvenor Museum.

Nearby, the Dewa Roman Experience is an interactive attraction with a reconstructed market place, barracks and bath house inviting you to experience the 'sights, sounds and smells of Roman Britain'.

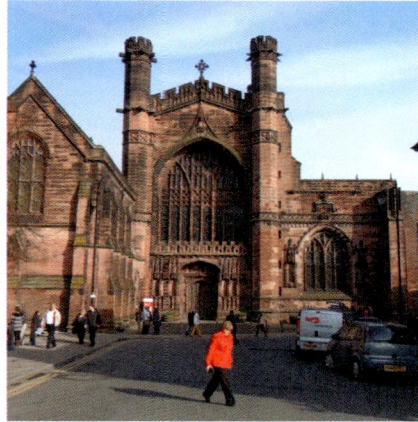

Chester Cathedral

Chester Cathedral spans nearly 1,000 years of history and also doubles as a venue for exhibitions and concerts. Chester Zoo is the largest zoo in the UK set in 110 acres of gardens and featuring more than 11,000 animals.

Chester's nightlife is eclectic with many traditional pubs and restaurants set in medieval buildings, as well as contemporary styled bars and clubs.

#18 Bristol

The city of Bristol is the largest in south western England and has a population of nearly half a million people who are known as 'Bristolians'. With a wide variety of attractions, good transport links and a gateway to Somerset, Devon and Cornwall, Bristol has a lot going for it.

The River Avon is a predominant feature of the city which is built around it. Some of Bristol's major attractions are situated on or near the river, including the Clifton Suspension Bridge and the Bristol Zoo.

Bristol was founded in the Saxon era before the 11th century AD, and was named 'Brycgstow' meaning 'the place at the bridge'. Evidence comes from silver coins bearing this name, which suggests the town had its own mint and was an important trading town.

The port grew in size during the next few centuries, exporting cloth and wheat, and importing wine and steel from Spain.

Bristol became a county in its own right in the 14th century, up until then it had been part of Gloucestershire. It remained an important English town until the Industrial Revolution when Manchester and Birmingham took the limelight.

Due to its coastal position, Bristol came under attack from German air raids during World War II and many heritage building were damaged. The city centre, therefore, predominantly features modern architecture and skyscrapers, though restoration of other more historic districts is an ongoing project in an effort to beautify the city.

If you're heading to Bristol for a short break or longer holiday, then you'll be spoiled for choice when it comes to attractions and activities. Music, film and art are all creative mediums strongly associated with the city.

One of England's most famous international artists, Banksy, hails from Bristol and has liberally left his mark on many of the public spaces, so a Banksy Walking Tour

is a must-do. Catching a live music gig in one of the many venues around the city is also a great way to spend an evening.

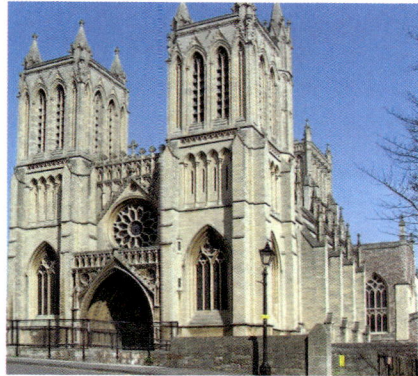

Bristol Cathedral

You can learn more about Bristol by visiting the M Shed, a contemporary museum dedicated to showcasing the history of the city and lives of its residents. Another popular museum is the At-Bristol, an interactive science center with loads of activities and exhibits aimed at families.

If you have time be sure to take in the Bristol Cathedral for its spectacular architecture; tours are available twice daily on Saturdays.

#19 Oxford

© Flickr / Jun

Oxford is best known as being home to Oxford University, one of the oldest academic institutions in the world, and is approximately an hour northwest by train from London. Predominantly a student city, the 39 University Colleges make up much of the architecture, with the spires of churches and chapels dominating the city's skyline. It was a student poet in the 19th century called Matthew Arnold who coined the phrase 'city of dreaming spires' which is still used to describe Oxford today. Many of Oxford's tourist activities are centered around the University, for example, the Colleges are open for public visits and Blackwell's on Broad Street, one of the oldest bookshops in the country, runs its own walking tours.

Oxford's settlement dates back to Saxon times to around 900 AD. It was first called 'Oxenaforda' which means 'Ford of the Oxen' or the place where oxen used to cross the river. Formal mention of the University in records isn't until the 12th century but teaching had been going on for at least a century beforehand. Students at this time lived in Halls of Residences, the only one remaining today being St. Edmund Hall which is dated back to 1225. Colleges replaced the Halls, and three of these, University College, Balliol and Merton are the oldest at Oxford dating from the the mid-13th century.

The 'city of dreaming spires' was at the forefront of modern technology during the 20th century with the establishment of Morris Motors Limited in Cowley on the outskirts of the city. With cars on the scene, major changes to the economy and society of Oxford took place, and the printing and publishing industries were also booming. Some of Oxford's most famous literary graduates include: Oscar Wilde, Percy Bysshe Shelley, John Donne, Lewis Carroll and W.H Auden.

Oxford architecture is unique in that it has examples of every period in English history since the Saxons, no mean feat. Suffice to say, a visit to Oxford is like taking a step back in time. Since the central city is pedestrianized, the best way to explore is by foot or by bicycle. There is a number of walking and bike tours available, some of them, such as Footprints Tours are run by students themselves.

© Wikimedia / Andrew Rivett

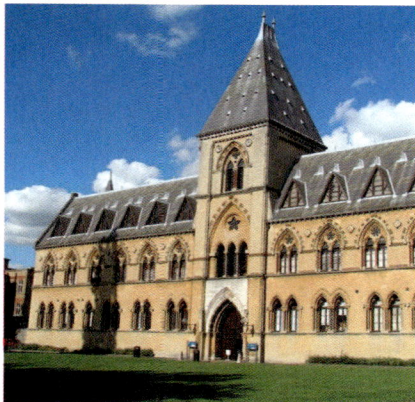

Oxford University Museum of Natural History

Take a rest after your tour in one of Oxfords many pubs, or go on the Oxford Pub Tour itself which takes in examples of some of England's oldest establishments. Many of the Colleges are open for public visits but do check the opening times, five of the most popular are: All Souls, Brasenose, Christ Church, Corpus Christi and Merton. Punting on the river is also a must-do activity in Oxford, so head to the Cherwell boathouse from which you can punt downstream, stopping for a picnic or a pint along the way.

#20 Durham

© Wikimedia / Steve F-E-Cameron

Last but not least on our list is Durham, an historic city in the northeast of England situated on the banks of the River Wear. Durham is located between Newcastle-upon-Tyne in the north and Darlington in the south, and is on the main train line between London and Edinburgh.

It has UNESCO World Heritage attractions, including a Norman cathedral and an 11th century castle which is the base for Durham University.

Visitors to Durham will be able to get spectacular views and great photo opportunities from this picturesque city.

Archaeologists have traced the settlement of the area to around 2000 BC and Durham itself to 995 AD. Records talk about a group of monks from Lindisfarne, a holy island off the coast, who were on a pilgrimage with the relics of St. Cuthbert.

They received a sign that they were to build a shrine to the saint and so an early version of Durham Cathedral, the first building of the city, was erected.

The shrine of St Cuthbert gave the newly founded city spiritual prominence during the medieval period because of its purported healing powers. Anyone visiting the shrine was said to be cured of their illness.

As well as its religious importance, as a city Durham was also in a strategic position to defend northern England against the Scottish and Durham Castle played a vital role in this respect.

Your first glimpse of the city if you're arriving by train will be of the Durham Cathedral and Durham Castle which dominate the skyline. These UNESCO World Heritage treasures are must-sees when first exploring the city.

The Cathedral, home to the shrine of St. Cuthbert, is open all year

round and free to enter; there are regular tours you can join also.

© Wikimedia / kanu101

University Boat Race with Durham Cathedral and Castle in the Background

Durham Castle is situated right next door and overlooks the river and city, it is a museum as well as a university residence with over 100 students; public guided tours are available during term time and university holidays.

Other popular attractions in Durham include the Market Place, one of the main shopping areas, the Beamish Museum, showcasing the city's history and the Bowes Museum, which holds contemporary exhibitions.

Map of the Places to Visit in England

#1 London

#2 Manchester

#3 York

#4 Liverpool

#5 Stonehenge

#6 Lake District

#7 Cornwall

#8 Bath

#9 Birmingham

#10 Cotswolds

#11 Brighton

#12 Devon

#13 Cambridge

#14 Blackpool

#15 Norfolk

#16 Suffolk

#17 Chester

#18 Bristol

#19 Oxford

#20 Durham

A Note to the Reader

Dear Reader

Thank you for your purchase of this Atsons Travel guide, we hope you have enjoyed reading it!

Please feel free to post an informative, unbiased review on Amazon so that others may benefit from your experience. Reviews help us spread the word of our books and attract fantastic customers such as yourselves.

Also your feedback is invaluable to us, as we work hard to serve you and continually improve our customers' experience.

Thanks in advance for your time and input, and thanks again for choosing Atsons!

Sincerely

Atsons Travel Guides

Printed in Great Britain
by Amazon